MW00962213

Copyright © 2017 by Gary Cartier

All rights reserved. No part of this publication may be reproduced, distributed, or transmitted in any form or by any means, including photocopying, recording, or other electronic or mechanical methods, without the prior written permission of the publisher, except in the case of brief quotations embodied in critical reviews and certain other noncommercial uses permitted by copyright law.

THE ULTIMATE BOOK OF

DAD

OVER 500 JOKES!

JOKES

GARY CARTIER

WHY CAN'T PIRATES FINISH THE ALPHABET?

BECAUSE THEY GOT LOST AT C!

WHAT DO YOU CALL A MONSTER WITH NO NECK?

THE LOST NECK MONSTER.

HOW DID THE DENTIST BECOME A BRAIN SURGEON?

HIS HAND SLIPPED.

WHY DO SHOEMAKERS GO TO HEAVEN?

BECAUSE THEY HAVE GOOD SOLES.

WHAT DID THE ILL COMIC SAY IN THE HOSPITAL?

"I'M HERE...ALL WEAK!"

HOW DID THE SKELETON KNOW WHAT WOULD HAPPEN NEXT?

HE COULD FEEL IT IN HIS BONES.

WHY DID THE MAN TAKE HIS STEPLADDER OUT?

BECAUSE HE NEVER GOT ALONG WITH HIS REAL LADDER.

A MAN TELLS HIS DOCTOR, "HELP ME. I'M ADDICTED TO TWITTER!"

THE DOCTOR REPLIES, "SORRY, I DON'T FOLLOW YOU."

HOW DO YOU KEEP A BAGEL FROM GETTING AWAY?

PUT LOX ON IT.

WHY CAN'T A WOMAN ASK HER BROTHER FOR HELP?

BECAUSE HE CAN'T BE A BROTHER AND ASSIST HER TOO.

WHY WERE ALL THE INK SPOTS CRYING?

THEIR FATHER WAS IN THE PEN.

WHY CAN'T YOU EXPLAIN PUNS TO KLEPTOMANIACS?

THEY ALWAYS TAKE THINGS LITERALLY.

HOW DO YOU TURN A DUCK INTO A SOUL SINGER?

PUT IT IN THE MICROWAVE UNTIL ITS BILL WHITHERS.

WHAT DID ONE CANNIBAL SAY TO THE OTHER WHILE EATING A CLOWN?

"DOES THIS TASTE FUNNY TO YOU?"

WHY SHOULD YOU RESPECT CLONES?

BECAUSE THEY'RE PEOPLE TWO.

WHAT DID ADAM SAY THE DAY BEFORE CHRISTMAS?

IT'S CHRISTMAS, EVE!

WHAT DID THE BALD MAN EXCLAIM WHEN HE RECEIVED A COMB FOR A PRESENT?

GEE, I'LL NEVER PART WITH IT!

WHO DELIVERS CHRISTMAS PRESENTS TO GOOD LITTLE SHARKS WHEN THEY'RE SLEEPING?

SANTA JAWS!

WHAT DO YOU GET WHEN YOU COMBINE A CHRISTMAS TREE WITH AN IPAD?

A PINEAPPLE.

WHY ARE COMET, CUPID, DONNER, AND BLITZEN ALWAYS WET?

BECAUSE THEY ARE RAIN DEER.

WHY DO WRITERS CONSTANTLY FEEL COLD?

BECAUSE THEY'RE SURROUNDED BY DRAFTS.

WHAT DOES CHARLES DICKENS KEEP IN HIS SPICE RACK?

THE BEST OF THYMES, THE WORST OF THYMES.

WHAT DID ONE BOAT SAY TO THE OTHER?

"ARE YOU UP FOR A LITTLE ROW-MANCE?"

WHICH IS FASTER, HEAT OR COLD?

HEAT, BECAUSE YOU CAN CATCH COLD!

WHY AREN'T DOGS GOOD DANCERS?

BECAUSE THEY HAVE TWO LEFT FEET!

WHY DO THEY TELL ACTORS TO "BREAK A LEG"?

BECAUSE EVERY PLAY HAS A CAST.

WHY ARE FROGS SO HAPPY?

THEY EAT WHATEVER BUGS THEM.

WHY ARE THERE NO ZIPPERS ON PANTS IN SYRIA?

IT'S A NO FLY ZONE.

WHAT DO YOU CALL SOMETHING THAT DOESN'T HAVE A MASS?

NOT CATHOLIC.

WHY SHOULD THE NUMBER 288 NEVER BE MENTIONED?

IT'S TWO GROSS.

WHAT DID AL GORE PLAY ON HIS GUITAR?

AN ALGORITHM.

WHY DO MATHEMATICIANS LIKE PARKS?

BECAUSE OF ALL THE NATURAL LOGS.

HAVE YOU HEARD ABOUT THE NEW RESTAURANT CALLED KARMA?

THERE'S NO MENU, YOU GET WHAT YOU DESERVE.

WHAT'S THE WORST PART ABOUT GETTING ELECTROCUTED?

IT HERTZ.

WHY DID THE MAN NAME IS PHONE "TITANIC"?

HE WANTED TO SEE THE TITANIC SYNCING.

WHY DID CHRISTOPHER COLUMBUS HATE POKER?

HE COULD NEVER BEAT THE STRAIGHTS OF MAGELLAN.

DID I TELL YOU ABOUT MY NEW BOWLING TEAM?

"I CAN'T BELIEVE IT'S NOT GUTTER."

WHAT DID THE TIN MAN SAY WHEN HE GOT RUN OVER?

CURSES, FOIL AGAIN!

WHAT DO BLACK FRIDAY SHOPPERS AND THE THANKSGIVING TURKEY HAVE IN COMMON?

THEY KNOW WHAT IT'S LIKE TO BE STUFFED AND THEN JAMMED INTO A SMALL PLACE.

WHY DID THE CHICKEN GO TO THE SEANCE?

TO GET TO THE OTHER SIDE.

WHAT HAPPENED TO THE MAN WHO TRIED TO SUE THE AIRPORT FOR MISPLACING HIS LUGGAGE?

HE LOST HIS CASE.

DID YOU HEAR ABOUT THE MAN WHO WAS ACCIDENTALLY BURIED ALIVE?

IT WAS A GRAVE MISTAKE.

WHAT HAPPENED TO THE MAN WHO RAN BEHIND THE CAR?

HE WAS EXHAUSTED.

WHAT HAPPENED TO THE MAN WHO RAN IN FRONT OF THE CAR?

HE WAS TIRED.

WHY DO FRENCH PEOPLE EAT SNAILS?

BECAUSE THEY DON'T LIKE FAST FOOD.

WHY ARE DOGS BAD STORYTELLERS?

BECAUSE THEY ONLY HAVE ONE TALE.

HOW MUCH ROOM SHOULD YOU GIVE FUNGI TO GROW?

AS MUSHROOM AS POSSIBLE.

HOW DO TREES GET ONLINE?

THEY JUST LOG IN.

WHY DID THE GIRL QUIT HER JOB AT THE DONUT FACTORY?

SHE WAS FED UP WITH THE HOLE BUSINESS.

HOW DO YOU LEARN HOW TO DRIVE A STICK SHIFT?

FIND A MANUAL.

HOW DID THE HIPSTER EAT HIS HOT DOG?

WITH A MAN BUN.

HOW DID THE LONG DISTANCE RELATIONSHIP GO?

SO FAR. SO GOOD.

WHAT DID THE BEACH SAY AS THE TIDE CAME IN?

LONG TIME, NO SEA.

DID YOU HEAR MY SONG ABOUT A TORTILLA?

ACTUALLY IT'S MORE OF A WRAP.

DID YOU HEAR ABOUT THE MAN WHO TRIED TO CATCH FOG?

HE MIST.

WHY DO HAMBURGERS GO TO THE GYM?

TO GET BETTER BUNS.

WHY SHOULDN'T YOU TELL A SECRET ON A FARM?

BECAUSE THE POTATOES HAVE EYES AND THE CORN HAS EARS.

WHAT DID THE LIBRARIAN SAY WHEN THE BOOKS WERE A MESS?

WE OUGHT TO BE ASHAMED OF OUR SHELVES!

WHAT DOES TIME FLY LIKE?

AN ARROW.

WHAT DOES FRUIT FLY LIKE?

A BANANA.

WHAT'S THE WORST PART ABOUT MOVIE THEATER CANDY PRICES?

THEY'RE ALWAYS RAISINET.

WHY SHOULDN'T YOU BECOME A VEGETARIAN?

IT'S A HUGE MISSED STEAK.

DID YOU HEAR I PUT ALL MY SPARE CASH INTO AN ORIGAMI BUSINESS?

IT FOLDED.

DID YOU HEAR ABOUT THE GUY WHO MADE A CAR OUT OF SPAGHETTI?

HE SAW HIS MOM AND RODE STRAIGHT PASTA.

WHAT DOES C.S. LEWIS KEEP AT THE BACK OF HIS WARDROBE?

NARNIA BUSINESS!

DID YOU HEAR ABOUT THE GUY WHO DIDN'T WANT A BRAIN TRANSPLANT?

HE CHANGED HIS MIND.

WHY DID THE WOMAN HIT HER HUSBAND WITH STRINGED INSTRUMENTS?

SHE HAD A HISTORY OF VIOLINS.

DID YOU HEAR ABOUT THE STOLEN TOILET?

THE POLICE HAVE NOTHING TO GO ON.

DID YOU HEAR ABOUT THE TWO SILK WORMS IN A RACE?

IT ENDED IN A TIE!

WHY DID THE MAN STAND ON ONE LEG AT THE BANK?

HE WAS CHECKING HIS BALANCE.

WHAT DO YOU CALL A FRENCHMAN WHO WEARS BEACH SANDALS?

PHILIPPE PHILLOPPE.

WHY SHOULD YOU NEVER USE A DULL PENCIL?

BECAUSE IT'S POINTLESS.

WHAT IS THE FUNNIEST PLANT IN THE DESERT?

THE YUCCA PLANT.

WHEN THE MYSTERY MACHINE BREAKS DOWN WHO HAS TO GO FOR HELP?

SCOOBY DO.

DID YOU HEAR ABOUT THE LUMBERJACK WHO WAS FIRED FOR CUTTING DOWN TOO MANY TREES?

HE SAW TOO MUCH.

WHAT DID THE BEAVER SAY TO THE TREE?

IT'S BEEN NICE GNAWING YOU.

WHY IS NO ONE FRIENDS WITH DRACULA?

BECAUSE HE'S A PAIN IN THE NECK.

WHY DON'T STEAK JOKES WORK? THEY'RE NEVER WELL DONE.	WHAT DO YOU CALL A FROG WITH NO LEGS? UN-HOPPY.
WHAT'S THE FUNNIEST CANDY BAR? SNICKERS.	WHAT DO YOU CALL A BEAR WITH NO SOCKS ON? BARE-FOOT.

WHAT'S THE DIFFERENCE BETWEEN IGNORANCE AND APATHY?

I DON'T KNOW AND I DON'T CARE.

WHERE DO HAMBURGERS GO TO DANCE?

THE MEATBALL.

WHY ARE PENGUINS SOCIALLY AWKWARD?

BECAUSE THEY CAN'T BREAK THE ICE.

WHY DID THE POOR MAN SELL YEAST?

TO RAISE SOME DOUGH.

WHAT DID THE FISHERMAN SAY TO THE MAGICIAN?

PICK A COD, ANY COD!

WHY DID THE CAN CRUSHER QUIT HIS JOB?

BECAUSE IT WAS SODA PRESSING.

WHY COULDN'T THE SESAME SEED LEAVE THE CASINO?

BECAUSE HE WAS ON A ROLL.

WHY DID THE YOGURT GO TO THE ART EXHIBIT?

BECAUSE IT WAS CULTURED.

DID THE DISAPPOINTED SMOKER GET EVERYTHING HE WANTED FOR CHRISTMAS?

CLOTHES, BUT NO CIGAR.

WHAT DO YOU CALL AN UNPREDICTABLE, OUT OF CONTROL PHOTOGRAPHER?

A LOOSE CANON.

HOW DO YOU IMPRESS A BAKER'S DAUGHTER?

BRING HER FLOURS.

DID YOU HEAR ABOUT THE SENSITIVE BURGLAR?

HE TAKES THINGS PERSONALLY.

WHAT DID THE BLANKET SAY TO THE BED?

DON'T WORRY, I'VE GOT YOU COVERED!

WHICH U.S. STATE HAS THE SMALLEST SOFT DRINKS?

MINI-SODA.

WHAT DID THE DUCK SAY TO THE BARTENDER?

PUT IT ON MY BILL.

WHAT KIND OF TEA IS HARD TO SWALLOW?

REALITY.

WHAT DO YOU CALL THE HEAVY BREATHING SOMEONE MAKES WHILE TRYING TO HOLD A YOGA POSE?

YOGA PANTS.

WHAT KIND OF DOGS LIKE CAR RACING?

LAP DOGS.

HOW DO HENS CHEER FOR THEIR TEAM?

THEY EGG THEM ON!

WHY WAS THE STUDENT'S REPORT CARD WET?

IT WAS BELOW C LEVEL!

WHY DID THE ROBBER TAKE A BATH?

BECAUSE HE WANTED TO MAKE A CLEAN GETAWAY!

WHAT LIGHTS UP A SOCCER STADIUM?

A SOCCER MATCH!

HOW DO YOU FIND A PRINCESS?

YOU FOLLOW THE FOOT PRINCE.

WHAT DID ONE TOILET SAY TO THE OTHER TOILET?

YOU LOOK FLUSHED!

IF APRIL SHOWERS BRING MAY FLOWERS, WHAT DO MAY FLOWERS BRING?

PILGRIMS.

HAVE YOU HEARD THEY DON'T NEED THE GOLDEN GATE BRIDGE ANY LONGER?

BECAUSE IT'S ALREADY LONG ENOUGH.

WHY DID THE COOKIE GO TO THE HOSPITAL?

BECAUSE HE FELT CRUMMY!

WHAT DID THE POLICEMAN SAY TO HIS SHIRT?

"YOU'RE UNDER A VEST."

WHAT DID ONE BIRD SAY TO THE OTHER CHEATING PARROT?

TOUCAN PLAY AT THAT GAME.

WHAT DO YOU DO WITH CHEMISTS WHEN THEY DIE?

BARIUM.

WHAT IS SANTA'S FAVOURITE PIZZA?

ONE THAT'S DEEP PAN, CRISP AND EVEN.

HOW DOES A MUPPET DIE?

APPARENTLY, IT KERMITS SUICIDE.

HOW MANY OPTOMETRISTS DOES IT TAKE TO CHANGE A LIGHT BULB? 1 OR 2? 1... OR 2?	HAVE YOU SEEN THE NEW MOVIE ABOUT TREES IN LOVE? IT'S PRETTY SAPPY.
WHY DO BEARS HAVE HAIRY COATS? FUR PROTECTION.	DID YOU HEAR ABOUT THE MAGIC TRACTOR? IT TURNED INTO A FIELD.

WHAT'S THE WORST THING ABOUT ANCIENT HISTORY CLASS? **THE TEACHERS TEND TO BABYLON.**	**WHAT DOES A HOUSE WEAR?** **A DRESS.**
HOW DO YOU MAKE ANTIFREEZE? **STEAL HER BLANKET.**	**DO YOU WANT TO HEAR A CHIMNEY JOKE?** **THE FIRST ONE'S ON THE HOUSE.**

WHAT HAPPENED TO THE COW THAT JUMPED OVER THE BARBED WIRE FENCE?

UDDER DESTRUCTION.

WHAT DID THE BUDDHIST ASK THE HOT DOG VENDOR?

"MAKE ME ONE WITH EVERYTHING."

WHO WONDERS IF THEIR UNIFORM MAKES THEM LOOK FAT?

AN INSECURITY GUARD.

HOW DOES THE MOON CUT HIS HAIR?

ECLIPSE IT!

WHAT SHOULD YOU DO IF YOU KEEP BURNING YOUR HAWAIIAN PIZZAS?

PUT IT ON ALOHA SETTING.

WHAT WOULD HAPPEN IF I SAW A BIG CAT ESCAPE HIS CAGE?

I'D PUMA PANTS.

HOW DO YOU COUNT COWS?

WITH A COWCULATOR!

WHAT'S A MARSUPIAL'S FAVOURITE COCKTAIL?

A PINA KOALA.

WHAT'S THE DIFFERENCE BETWEEN IN-LAWS AND OUTLAWS? OUTLAWS ARE WANTED.	WHAT OFTEN GETS OVERLOOKED? FENCES.
WHY COULDN'T THE MAN PLANT FLOWERS? HE HADN'T BOTANY.	WHAT'S THE LEADING CAUSE OF DRY SKIN? TOWELS.

WHAT DAYS ARE THE STRONGEST?

SATURDAY AND SUNDAY, THE REST ARE WEEK DAYS.

HAVE YOU EVER HEARD OF A MUSIC GROUP CALLED CELLOPHANE?

THEY MOSTLY WRAP.

WHAT DO YOU CALL DAVID AFTER HE LOSES HIS ID?

DAV.

WHY ARE SKELETONS SO CALM?

BECAUSE NOTHING GETS UNDER THEIR SKIN.

WHAT'S THE DIFFERENCE BETWEEN AN AFRICAN ELEPHANT AND AN INDIAN ELEPHANT?

ABOUT 5000 MILES.

WHAT DID THE DADDY TOMATO SAY TO THE BABY TOMATO?

CATCH UP!

WHAT'S THE BEST DAMN PROGRAM ON TV?

A DOCUMENTARY ABOUT BEAVERS.

WHERE DOES BATMAN GO TO DO HIS BUSINESS?

THE BATROOM.

WHAT DO YOU CALL A GROUP OF KILLER WHALES PLAYING INSTRUMENTS?

AN ORCA-STRA.

WHY DID THE OCTOPUS BEAT THE SHARK IN A FIGHT?

BECAUSE IT WAS WELL-ARMED.

WHAT DID THE BARTENDER SAY TO THE JUMPER CABLE?

"I'LL SERVE YOU, BUT DON'T START ANYTHING."

WHERE CAN YOU GET CHICKEN BROTH IN BULK?

THE STOCK MARKET.

HOW CAN YOU TELL IF A ANT IS A BOY OR A GIRL?

THEY'RE ALL GIRLS, OTHERWISE THEY'D BE UNCLES.

WHERE DID THE ONE-LEGGED WAITRESS WORK?

IHOP!

WHY DID THE COOKIE CRY?

BECAUSE HIS FATHER WAS A WAFER SO LONG!

DID I TELL YOU THE TIME I FELL IN LOVE DURING A BACKFLIP?

I WAS HEELS OVER HEAD.

WHAT DO YOU CALL A HEN LOOKING AT OUR LETTUCE?

CHICKEN SEES OUR SALAD.

WHY DID THE MAN BECOME A PROFESSIONAL LEAF COLLECTOR?

HE STARTED RAKING IT IN.

WHAT DO YOU GET IF YOU STAND BETWEEN TWO LLAMAS?

LLAMANATED.

WHY DID THE MAN LOVE THE ROTATION OF THE EARTH?

BECAUSE IT REALLY MADE HIS DAY.

WHAT DO YOU CALL A MAN WITH NO ARMS AND NO LEGS LYING IN FRONT OF YOUR DOOR?

MATT.

WHAT LIES AT THE BOTTOM OF THE OCEAN AND TWITCHES?

A NERVOUS WRECK.

WHAT DID THE FROG WHO WAS ALWAYS BEING BOSSED AROUND SAY?

I JUST DO WHAT I'M TOAD.

WHAT DID THE PIRATE SAY ON HIS 80TH BIRTHDAY?

AYE, MATEY!

DO AUSTRALIANS TAKE CREAM?

NO THEY JUST HAVE COFFEE, MATE.

WHY WAS THE KING ONE FOOT TALL?

BECAUSE HE WAS A RULER.

WHAT DO YOU CALL TWO CARNIVORES FIGHTING?

A BEEF.

WHAT DID THE WOMAN SAY WHEN SHE SAW HER GREY HAIRS?

"I FEEL LIKE DYEING."

WHAT DO YOU GET WHEN YOU CROSS SPEEDY GONZALES WITH A COUNTRY SINGER? ARRIBA MCENTIRE.	WHAT IS A TREE'S FAVORITE DRINK? ROOT BEER.
WHERE DOES BAD LIGHT GO? PRISM.	WHAT MUSIC ARE BALLOONS SCARED OF? POP MUSIC.

DID YOU HEAR ABOUT THE GHOST COMEDIAN?

HE WAS BOOED OFF STAGE.

WHAT DO YOU GET IF YOU A CROSS A CARD GAME WITH A TYPHOON?

BRIDGE OVER TROUBLED WATER.

HOW DO SPIDERS COMMUNICATE?

THE WORLD WIDE WEB.

DID YOU HEAR ABOUT THE LIMO DRIVER WHO WENT 25 YEARS WITHOUT A CUSTOMER?

ALL THAT TIME AND NOTHING TO CHAUFFEUR IT.

WHAT DO YOU CALL A SNOWMAN WITH A SIX PACK? **AN ABDOMINAL SNOWMAN.**	**WHAT'S THE DIFFERENCE BETWEEN ROAST BEEF AND PEA SOUP?** **YOU CAN'T PEA SOUP.**
WHAT DO YOU CALL A CRUSHED ANGLE? **A RECTANGLE.**	**WHAT DO YOU CALL LEFTOVER ALIENS?** **EXTRA TERRESTRIALS.**

WHAT DO BULLS DO WHEN THEY GO SHOPPING? THEY CHARGE.	**WHERE DO BOATS GO WHEN THEY GET SICK?** THE DOCK.
WHAT DID ONE PLATE SAY TO THE OTHER? DINNER'S ON ME.	**WHAT KIND OF FLOWER DOESN'T SLEEP AT NIGHT?** THE DAY-ZZZ.

WHAT DO YOU GIVE A DOG WITH A FEVER?

MUSTARD, IT'S THE BEST THING FOR A HOT DOG.

WHAT DID THE DIGITAL WATCH SAY TO THE GRANDFATHER CLOCK?

LOOK GRAMPS, NO HANDS!

WHAT DO CATS EAT FOR BREAKFAST?

MICE CRISPIES.

HOW DO YOU COMMUNICATE WITH A FISH?

DROP HIM A LINE.

WHAT IS AN ASTRONAUT'S FAVORITE PLACE ON A KEYBOARD? THE SPACE BAR.	WHY IS BASKETBALL SUCH A MESSY SPORT? ALL THE DRIBBLING.
WHAT EXAM DO YOUNG WITCHES HAVE TO PASS? A SPELL-ING TEST.	WHAT RUNS BUT DOESN'T GET ANYWHERE? A REFRIGERATOR.

WHY WAS THE MATH BOOK SAD? BECAUSE IT HAD TOO MANY PROBLEMS.	WHY DO WATERMELONS HAVE FANCY WEDDINGS? BECAUSE THEY CANTALOUPE.
DID YOU HEAR ABOUT THE TWO BED BUGS WHO MET IN THE MATTRESS? THEY GOT MARRIED IN THE SPRING.	HOW DO BASEBALL PLAYERS STAY COOL? THEY SIT NEXT TO THEIR FANS.

WHAT DID THE HAMBURGER NAME HIS DAUGHTER? PATTY.	WHAT DO YOU CALL A TEACHER WHO NEVER PASSES GAS IN PUBLIC? A PRIVATE TUTOR.
WHAT KIND OF EGG DID THE BAD CHICKEN LAY? A DEVILED EGG.	HOW DO YOU REPAIR A BROKEN TOMATO? TOMATO PASTE.

WHY DID THE MAN LOSE HIS JOB AT THE ORANGE JUICE FACTORY?

HE COULDN'T CONCENTRATE!

WHAT DO YOU CALL A SOUTH AMERICAN GIRL WHO IS ALWAYS IN A HURRY?

URGENT-TINA.

HOW DID THE FARMER MEND HIS PANTS?

WITH CABBAGE PATCHES.

WHAT DID THE TAILOR THINK OF HIS NEW JOB?

IT WAS SEW SEW.

WHAT DO YOU CALL A MAGICIAN ON A PLANE? A FLYING SORCERER.	WHAT KIND OF SHORTS DO CLOUDS WEAR? THUNDERWEAR.
WHAT HAPPENED TO THE WOODEN CAR WITH WOODEN WHEELS AND WOODEN ENGINE? IT WOODEN GO!	WHICH MONTH DO SOLDIERS HATE MOST? THE MONTH OF MARCH.

DID YOU HEAR ABOUT THE LUMBERJACK WHO DIED?

THE POLICE ARE CALLING IT AN AXE-IDENT.

WHY DOES A MILKING STOOL HAVE ONLY 3 LEGS?

BECAUSE THE COW HAS THE UDDER.

WHAT KIND OF DRIVER NEVER GETS A PARKING TICKET?

A SCREWDRIVER.

DID YOU HEAR ABOUT THE SICK JUGGLER?

HE COULDNT STOP THROWING UP.

WHAT DO YOU CALL A NERVOUS JAVELIN THROWER? SHAKESPEARE.	DID YOU HEAR ABOUT THE ASTRONAUT WHO STEPPED ON CHEWING GUM? HE GOT STUCK IN ORBIT.
DID YOU HEAR ABOUT THE CALENDAR THIEF? HE GOT 12 MONTHS.	WHAT HAPPENS IF LIFE GIVES YOU MELONS? YOU'RE DYSLEXIC.

WHAT HAPPENED WHEN THE SKUNK WALKED INTO THE COURTROOM?

THERE WAS ODOR IN THE COURT.

WHAT DO YOU CALL MOM AND DAD GHOSTS?

TRANSPARENTS.

WHY DID THE TOMATO TURN RED?

IT SAW THE SALAD DRESSING.

WHAT STREETS DO GHOSTS HAUNT?

DEAD ENDS.

WHY DO SEAGULLS FLY OVER THE SEA?

BECAUSE IF THEY FLEW OVER THE BAY THEY WOULD BE BAGELS.

WHAT DO YOU CALL AN 80S POP BAND WITH A SCOOP OF ICE CREAM?

DEPECHE A LA MODE.

WHAT DO YOU CALL A GROUP OF MEN WAITING FOR A HAIRCUT?

A BARBER-CUE.

WHAT DO YOU CALL A FROZEN DOG?

A PUPSICLE.

WHAT DID THE BLANKET SAY TO THE BED?

DON'T WORRY, I'VE GOT YOU COVERED.

WHY COULDN'T THE PIRATE PLAY CARDS?

BECAUSE HE WAS SITTING ON THE DECK.

WHAT DID ONE ELEVATOR SAY TO THE OTHER ELEVATOR?

I THINK I'M COMING DOWN WITH SOMETHING.

DID YOU HEAR THE ONE ABOUT THE GEOLOGIST?

HE TOOK HIS WIFE FOR GRANITE.

WHY DID TONY GO OUT WITH A PRUNE?

BECAUSE HE COULDN'T FIND A DATE.

DID YOU HEAR ABOUT THE GUY WHO GOT HIT IN THE HEAD WITH A CAN OF SODA?

HE WAS LUCKY IT WAS A SOFT DRINK.

WHAT DID THE LITTLE MOUNTAIN SAY TO THE BIG MOUNTAIN?

HI, CLIFF.

WHAT WASHES UP ON VERY SMALL BEACHES?

MICROWAVES.

WHAT DO YOU CALL A BEAR WITH NO TEETH? A GUMMY BEAR.	WHAT DO YOU CALL A RELIGIOUS PERSON THAT SLEEP WALKS? A ROMAN CATHOLIC.
WHERE DO SNOWMEN KEEP THEIR MONEY? IN SNOW BANKS.	WHAT DO YOU CALL A MUSICIAN WITH PROBLEMS? A TREBLED MAN.

WHAT DO YOU CALL A COW WITH A TWITCH?

BEEF JERKY.

DID YOU HEAR THE JOKE ABOUT THE ROOF?

NEVER MIND, IT'S OVER YOUR HEAD.

WHAT THREE CANDIES CAN YOU FIND IN EVERY SCHOOL?

NERDS, DUMDUMS, AND SMARTIES.

WHAT DO YOU CALL A BEE THAT LIVES IN AMERICA?

USB.

WHAT DO YOU CALL SOMEONE WHO IS AFRAID OF SANTA?

A CLAUS-TROPHOBIC.

WHY DID THE CROSS-EYED TEACHER LOSE HER JOB?

SHE COULDN'T CONTROL HER PUPILS.

WHAT IS THE BEST SEASON FOR TRAMPOLINING?

SPRINGTIME.

WHAT DO YOU CALL A LAUGHING MOTORCYCLE?

A YAMAHAHAHA.

WHY IS ENGLAND THE WETTEST COUNTRY?	WHY DID THE MAN PUT HIS MONEY IN THE FREEZER?
BECAUSE THE QUEEN HAS REIGNED THERE FOR YEARS.	HE WANTED COLD HARD CASH.
WHY ARE PIRATES CALLED PIRATES?	WHY DID THE COMPUTER GO TO THE DOCTOR?
CAUSE THEY ARRRRR.	IT HAD A VIRUS.

HOW DO YOU MAKE HOLY WATER? BOIL THE HELL OUT OF IT.	WHAT KIND OF JOKES DO YOU MAKE IN THE SHOWER? CLEAN JOKES.
WHERE DO BEES GO TO THE BATHROOM? AT THE BP STATION.	HOW DO YOU DROWN A HIPSTER IN THE MAINSTREAM.

WHAT DID THE FEMUR SAY TO THE PATELLA?

I KNEED YOU SO LET'S BLOW THIS JOINT.

WHAT DID THE BURGER SAY TO THE BUN?

LETTUCE GET TOGETHER AND KETCHUP.

WHAT IS IT CALLED WHEN A CAT WINS A DOG SHOW?

CAT-HAS-TROPHY.

DID YOU HEAR ABOUT THE SHAMPOO SHORTAGE IN JAMAICA?

IT'S DREAD-FULL.

WHAT DO YOU CALL A REALLY BIG PSYCHIC? A FOUR CHIN TELLER.	WHERE DO CRAYONS GO ON VACATION? COLOR-ADO.
WHY DID THE BELT GET ARRESTED? HE HELD UP A PAIR OF PANTS.	WHAT DO LAWYERS WEAR TO COURT? LAWSUITS.

DID YOU HEAR ABOUT THAT NEW BROOM? IT'S SWEEPING THE NATION.	WHAT DID MISSISSIPPI BUY VIRGINIA? A NEW JERSEY.
WHAT DID DELAWARE? I DON'T KNOW, ALASKA.	WHAT DO YOU GET FROM A PAMPERED COW? SPOILED MILK.

HOW DID DARTH VADER KNOW WHAT LUKE GOT HIM FOR CHRISTMAS?

HE FELT HIS PRESENTS.

WHAT DID ONE WALL SAY TO THE OTHER?

MEET YOU AT THE CORNER.

WHAT DO YOU CALL A BELT MADE OUT OF WATCHES?

A WAIST OF TIME.

WHAT DO YOU CALL A COMPUTER THAT SINGS?

ADELE.

WHAT DO YOU DO WHEN THERE'S A SINK STANDING OUTSIDE YOUR DOOR?

YOU LET THAT SINK IN.

WHAT'S THE DIFFERENCE BETWEEN A CROCODILE AND AN ALLIGATOR?

ONE YOU'LL SEE IN A WHILE AND THE OTHER YOU'LL SEE LATER.

WHY CAN'T ZOO ANIMALS TAKE TESTS?

THERE ARE TOO MANY CHEETAHS.

WHAT DID ONE BEAN SAY TO THE OTHER BEAN?

HOW YOU BEAN?

WHAT DID THE OVERLY EXCITED GARDENER DO WHEN SPRING FINALLY ARRIVED?

HE WET HIS PLANTS.

HOW MUCH DOES A HIPSTER WEIGH?

AN INSTAGRAM.

WHY DOES WALDO WEAR A STRIPED SHIRT?

BECAUSE HE DOESN'T WANT TO BE SPOTTED!

WHAT'S GREEN AND SINGS?

ELVIS PARSLEY.

WHAT KIND OF PICTURES DO TURTLES TAKE?

SHELLFIES.

WHAT DID THE RED LIGHT SAY TO THE GREEN LIGHT?

DON'T LOOK, I'M CHANGING!

WHAT DO YOU CALL A POOR NEIGHBORHOOD IN ITALY?

A SPAGHETTO.

HOW DO CRAZY PEOPLE GET THROUGH A FOREST?

THEY TAKE THE PSYCHO-PATH.

WHAT'S THE BEST WAY TO CARVE WOOD? WHITTLE BY WHITTLE.	WHY DID THE PICTURE GO TO JAIL? BECAUSE HE WAS FRAMED.
WHAT TYPE OF MUSIC DO MUMMIES LISTEN TO? WRAP MUSIC.	WHAT DID THE FINGER SAY TO THE THUMB? I'M IN GLOVE WITH YOU.

WHAT DID ONE SNOWMAN SAY TO THE OTHER SNOWMAN?

"DO YOU SMELL CARROTS?"

WHAT'S LARGE, GREY, AND DOESN'T MATTER?

AN IRRELEPHANT.

WHAT DOES A BABY COMPUTER CALL HIS FATHER?

DATA.

WHAT DO HILLBILLIES DRINK OUT OF?

HICCUPS.

WHY DID THE CYCLOPS CLOSE HIS SCHOOL? BECAUSE HE ONLY HAD ONE PUPIL.	WHY DID THE MAN SELL HIS VACUUM? IT DID NOTHING BUT COLLECT DUST.
WHAT DO SPRINTERS EAT BEFORE A RACE? NOTHING, THEY JUST FAST.	HOW DO SNAILS FIGHT? THEY SLUG IT OUT.

WHAT DID JAY-Z CALL HIS GIRLFRIEND BEFORE THEY WERE MARRIED?

FEYONCÉ.

WHY DO VAMPIRES BELIEVE EVERYTHING YOU TELL THEM?

BECAUSE THEY'RE SUCKERS.

DOES ANYONE NEED AN ARK?

BECAUSE I NOAH GUY.

WHAT'S RED AND BAD FOR YOUR TEETH?

A BRICK.

WHAT DO YOU CALL A PERSON IN A TREE WITH A BRIEFCASE?

A BRANCH MANAGER.

WHAT'S BROWN AND SOUNDS LIKE A BELL?

DUNG.

WHAT DO YOU GIVE A SICK BIRD?

TWEETMENT.

WHAT DO YOU CALL A SNOBBISH PRISONER GOING DOWN THE STAIRS?

A CONDESCENDING CON DESCENDING.

WHY COULDN'T THE LIFEGUARD SEE THE HIPPIE?	WHAT DID THE MAN SAY BEFORE HE KICKED THE BUCKET?
HE WAS TOO FAR OUT, MAN.	"HOW FAR DO YOU THINK I CAN KICK THIS BUCKET?"
HOW DO YOU FIND WILL SMITH IN THE SNOW?	HOW MUCH DO HUMAN BONES WEIGH?
LOOK FOR FRESH PRINTS.	A SKELE-TON.

WHAT DID THE BIG CHIMNEY SAY TO THE LITTLE CHIMNEY?

"YOU ARE TOO YOUNG TO SMOKE."

IF ONE IS SINGLE AND TWO IS A COUPLE AND THREE IS A CROWD, WHAT IS FOUR AND FIVE?

9.

WHAT DO YOU CALL A FAIRY THAT DOESN'T BATHE?

STINKERBELL.

WHEN IS IT A GOOD TIME TO EAT A WINDOW?

WHEN IT'S JAMMED.

WHEN WERE
VOWELS
INVENTED?

WHEN U AND I
WERE BORN.

WHAT HAS FOUR
WHEELS AND
FLIES?

A GARBAGE
TRUCK.

WHAT'S ORANGE
AND SOUNDS
LIKE A PARROT?

A CARROT.

WHAT DO YOU
CALL A CAR
THAT EVERYONE
CAN BUY?

AFFORD.

WHERE DO ANIMALS GO WHEN THEIR TAILS FALL OFF? THE RETAIL STORE.	**WHAT DO YOU CALL A LOST WOLF?** A WHERE-WOLF.
HOW DOES A TRAIN EAT? IT GOES CHEW CHEW.	**DID YOU HEAR ABOUT THE MAGICIAN WHO WAS DRIVING DOWN THE STREET?** HE TURNED INTO A DRIVEWAY.

WHAT TIME DID THE MAN GET TO WIMBLEDON?	WHAT KIND OF BAGEL CAN FLY?
TENNISH.	A PLAIN BAGEL.
WHAT DO YOU CALL A ZOO WITH ONLY ONE DOG?	HOW MANY SOUTH AMERICANS DOES IT TAKE TO CHANGE A LIGHTBULB?
A SHIH TZU.	A BRAZILIAN.

HOW DO YOU GET RID OF AN ITCH? START FROM SCRATCH.	WHY CAN'T ELSA HAVE A BALLOON? BECAUSE SHE'LL LET IT GO.
HOW CAN YOU TELL IF A CLOCK IS HUNGRY? IT GOES BACK FOUR SECONDS.	WHAT DO YOU CALL A BABY MONKEY? A CHIMP OFF THE OLD BLOCK.

WHAT DO YOU CALL A PRIEST THAT BECOMES A LAWYER?

A FATHER-IN-LAW.

WHAT DID THE POLICE SAY WHEN THEY RAIDED A SEAFOOD RESTAURANT?

DON'T MOVE A MUSSEL.

WHAT HAPPENED WHEN THE MAN LOST HIS JOB AT THE MINT FACTORY?

HE WENT ABSOLUTELY MENTHOL.

WHAT DID THE CASKET SAY TO THE OTHER SICK CASKET?

IS THAT YOU COFFIN?

WHAT HAPPENS IF A FROG PARKS ILLEGALLY? HE GETS TOAD.	**WHY DID THE BARBER WIN THE RACE?** HE KNEW A SHORTCUT.
WHAT JAM CAN'T YOU EAT? TRAFFIC.	**HOW MUCH DID THE PIRATE'S NEW EARRINGS COST HIM?** A BUCCANEER.

WHAT DO YOU CALL A PERSON WHO TELLS DAD JOKES BUT HAS NO KIDS? A FAUX PA.	WHY CAN'T TWO ELEPHANTS GO SWIMMING? BECAUSE THEY ONLY HAVE ONE PAIR OF TRUNKS.
WHAT RHYMES WITH ORANGE? NO IT DOESN'T.	WHY DO CHICKEN COOPS ONLY HAVE TWO DOORS? BECAUSE IF THEY HAD FOUR DOORS, THEY'D BE CHICKEN SEDANS.

WHAT DO YOU CALL AN OLD PERSON WITH REALLY GOOD HEARING? DEAF DEFYING.	WHY COULDN'T THE MAN STOP PRETENDING TO BE BUTTER? HE WAS ON A ROLL.
HOW DOES DARTH VADER LIKE HIS TOAST? ON THE DARK SIDE.	WHERE DO YOU LEARN TO MAKE ICE CREAM? AT SUNDAE SCHOOL.

WHY DID THE MAN DELAY HIS TRIP TO MOSCOW?

THERE WAS NO POINT RUSSIAN INTO THINGS.

HOW MANY EARS DOES CAPTAIN KIRK HAVE?

THREE: THE LEFT EAR, THE RIGHT EAR, AND THE FINAL FRONTIER.

WHY WAS THE CALENDAR AFRAID?

ITS DAYS WERE NUMBERED.

WHY WAS THE ENERGIZER BUNNY ARRESTED?

BATTERY.

WHAT HAPPENS IF YOU EAT YEAST AND SHOE POLISH?

EVERY MORNING YOU'LL RISE AND SHINE!

WHAT DID THE DOCTOR SAY TO THE MAN ABOUT HIS BLADDER INFECTION?

URINE TROUBLE.

WHAT DO YOU CALL AN ALLIGATOR IN A VEST?

AN INVESTIGATOR.

HOW DID THE WOMAN KNOW HER WEDDING WAS BEAUTIFUL?

EVEN THE CAKE WAS IN TIERS.

WANNA HEAR TWO SHORT JOKES AND A LONG JOKE?

JOKE, JOKE, JOOOOOOOOOOOKE.

WHY DIDN'T THE WRESTLER GET A NEW HAIRCUT?

HE HAD TO MULLET OVER.

WHAT DO YOU CALL SANTA'S HELPERS?

SUBORDINATE CLAUSES.

WHY DOES PETER PAN ALWAYS FLY?

BECAUSE HE NEVERLANDS.

WHAT DID THE LEFT EYE SAY TO THE RIGHT EYE?

BETWEEN YOU AND ME, SOMETHING SMELLS.

WHY DO BANANAS NEED SUNSCREEN?

BECAUSE THEY PEEL.

WANT TO HEAR MY PIZZA JOKE?

NEVER MIND, IT'S TOO CHEESY.

WANT TO HEAR A WORD I JUST MADE UP?

PLAGIARISM.

WHAT'S A PIRATE'S FAVORITE LETTER?

YOU THINK IT'S R BUT IT'S THE C.

WHAT DID THE GREEN GRAPE SAY TO THE PURPLE GRAPE?

"BREATHE! BREATHE!"

HAVE YOU HEARD ABOUT CORDUROY PILLOWS?

THEY'RE MAKING HEADLINES.

WHAT DO ALEXANDER THE GREAT AND KERMIT THE FROG HAVE IN COMMON?

SAME MIDDLE NAME.

HOW DOES NASA ORGANIZE A PARTY?

THEY PLANET.

WHY AREN'T KOALAS ACTUAL BEARS?

THEY DON'T MEET THE KOALAFICATIONS.

WHAT DO YOU GET WHEN YOU CROSS A DYSLEXIC, AN INSOMNIAC, AND AN AGNOSTIC?

SOMEONE WHO LAYS AWAKE AT NIGHT WONDERING IF THERE IS A DOG.

WHAT DO YOU CALL BEARS WITH NO EARS?

B.

WHERE DOES THE GENERAL KEEP HIS ARMIES?

IN HIS SLEEVIES.

DID YOU HEAR ABOUT THE GUY WHO INVENTED THE KNOCK KNOCK JOKE?

HE WON THE NO BELL PRIZE.

DID YOU HEAR ABOUT THEY GUY WHO WAS AFRAID OF ELEVATORS?

HE'S TAKING STEPS TO AVOID THEM.

WHAT TIME OF DAY WAS ADAM BORN?

A LITTLE BEFORE EVE.

WHAT DID THE GRAPE DO WHEN HE GOT STEPPED ON? HE LET OUT A LITTLE WINE.	DID YOU HEAR THE JOKE ABOUT THE GERMAN SAUSAGE? IT WAS THE WURST.
DID YOU HEAR ABOUT THE CHEESE FACTORY EXPLOSION IN FRANCE? THERE WAS NOTHING LEFT BUT DE BRIE.	WHAT DO YOU CALL A MAN WITH A RUBBER TOE? ROBERTO.

WANT TO HEAR A JOKE ABOUT CONSTRUCTION?

SORRY, I'M STILL WORKING ON IT.

DID YOU HEAR ABOUT THE MOTHER WHO GAVE BIRTH IN THE SKY?

THE BABY WAS AIRBORNE.

WHY DID THE SCARECROW WIN AN AWARD?

BECAUSE HE WAS OUTSTANDING IN HIS FIELD.

WHAT DO YOU CALL CHEESE THAT ISN'T YOURS?

NACHO CHEESE.

HOW DOES A PENGUIN BUILD ITS HOUSE? IGLOOS IT TOGETHER.	WHAT DO YOU CALL A FAKE NOODLE? AN IMPASTA.
WHY DID THE COFFEE FILE A POLICE REPORT? IT GOT MUGGED.	HOW MANY APPLES GROW ON A TREE? ALL OF THEM.

WHAT DID THE BUFFALO SAY TO HIS SON WHEN HE DROPPED HIM OFF AT SCHOOL?

BISON.

WHY DID THE CRAB NEVER SHARE?

BECAUSE HE'S SHELLFISH.

WHY WASN'T THE WOMAN HAPPY WITH THE VELCRO SHE BOUGHT?

IT WAS A TOTAL RIPOFF.

WHAT DOES AN ANGRY PEPPER DO?

IT GETS JALAPEÑO YOUR FACE.

WHY CAN'T YOU HEAR A PTERODACTYL GO TO THE BATHROOM? BECAUSE THE PEE IS SILENT.	**CAN FEBRUARY MARCH?** NO, BUT APRIL MAY.
WHAT DOES A VEGETARIAN ZOMBIE EAT? GRAINS.	**WHAT DO YOU CALL A LONELY CHEESE?** PROVOLONE.

WHAT DO YOU GET WHEN YOU CROSS A SNOWMAN WITH A VAMPIRE? FROSTBITE.	**WHAT DO YOU CALL A FISH WITH TWO KNEES?** A "TWO-KNEE" FISH.
WHAT IS THE LOUDEST PET YOU CAN BUY? A TRUMPET.	**WHY DIDN'T THE VAMPIRE ATTACK TAYLOR SWIFT?** SHE HAD BAD BLOOD.

WHAT DO YOU CALL A DOG THAT CAN DO MAGIC? A LABRACADABRADOR.	**WHY COULDN'T THE BIKE STAND UP BY ITSELF?** IT WAS TWO TIRED.
HOW MANY TICKLES DOES IT TAKE TO MAKE AN OCTOPUS LAUGH? TEN-TICKLES.	**WHAT DO PRISONERS USE TO CALL EACH OTHER?** CELL PHONES.

WHAT DO YOU CALL A COW WITH TWO LEGS? LEAN BEEF.	**WHAT DO YOU CALL A COW WITH NO LEGS?** GROUND BEEF.
WHY SHOULDN'T YOU TRUST ATOMS? THEY MAKE UP EVERYTHING.	**DID YOU HEAR ABOUT THE CIRCUS FIRE?** IT WAS IN TENTS!

WHAT DID THE TERMITE SAY WHEN HE WALKED INTO THE BAR? "IS THE BAR TENDER HERE?"	WHAT DO YOU CALL A COW THAT JUST GAVE BIRTH? DECAFFEINATED.
IF YOU'RE GOING OUT TO DINNER, HOW SHOULD YOU LOOK? WITH YOUR EYES.	ARE YOU ALRIGHT? NO, I'M HALF LEFT.

WHAT DO YOU CALL A FACTORY THAT MAKES OK PRODUCTS?

A SATISFACTORY.

WHAT DO YOU CALL A PERSON WHO SEES A ROBERRY AT AN APPLE STORE?

IWITNESS.

DID YOU HEAR ABOUT THE PIECE OF PAPER?

IT'S SO TEARABLE.

WHERE WERE THE FIRST FRENCH FRIES MADE?

GREECE.

DID YOU HEAR ABOUT THE GUY WHO INVENTED ALTOIDS?

THEY SAY HE MADE A MINT.

WHY DID THE CLYDESDALE GIVE THE PONY A GLASS OF WATER?

BECAUSE HE WAS A LITTLE HORSE!

WHAT IS BEETHOVEN'S FAVORITE FRUIT?

A BA-NA-NA-NA.

WHAT IS THE MOST POPULAR BLOOD TYPE?

RED.

WHAT TIME DID THE MAN GO TO THE DENTIST?

TOOTH HURT-Y.

WHAT HAPPENED WHEN 1 AND 20 PLAYED A GAME TOGETHER?

21.

WHY DID THE POLICE OFFICER ARREST THE CHICKEN?

HE SUSPECTED FOWL PLAY.

HOW DO YOU STOP EATING AT THANKSGIVING?

QUIT COLD TURKEY.

WHY DID THE ROCK BAND HIRE THE TURKEY?

HE CAME WITH DRUMSTICKS.

WHERE DO NEW YORK DADS GO TO GET NEW JOKES?

CORNY ISLAND.

WHEN IS A DOOR NOT A DOOR?

WHEN IT IS AJAR.

WHY DIDN'T THE BARTENDER SERVE THE WIG?

IT FORGOT TOUPEE.

A MAN WALKS INTO A LIBRARY AND ASKS, "CAN I HAVE A CHEESEBURGER?"

THE LIBRARIAN SAYS, "SIR, THIS IS A LIBRARY." THE MAN WHISPERS, "CAN I HAVE A CHEESEBURGER?"

WHAT ENDS WITH AN E AND HAS LOTS OF LETTERS IN IT?

POST OFFICE.

WHAT KIND OF NEWS DOES THE OCEAN FOLLOW?

CURRENT.

WHICH CAT IS THE MOST DELICIOUS?

KIT KAT.

WHY DID C-3PO GET LOST? HE WENT ON AN R2-DTOUR.	**I HAVE 4 EYES, 2 MOUTHS AND 5 EARS. WHAT AM I?** UGLY.
WHY DO GOLFERS WEAR TWO PAIRS OF SOCKS? IN CASE THEY GET A HOLE IN ONE.	**WHAT DO YOU CALL A BABY TURKEY?** A GOBLET.

WHAT DO YOU CALL A NOSE THAT CAN FORESEE THE FUTURE?

NOSTRILDAMUS.

WHAT DID ONE STRAWBERRY SAY TO THE OTHER?

IF YOU WEREN'T SO FRESH, WE WOULDN'T BE IN THIS JAM.

WHAT DO YOU CALL A WOMAN WHO CAN'T STAND UP STRAIGHT?

EILEEN.

WHAT DO MERMAIDS WASH THEIR FINS WITH?

TIDE.

WHAT DID ONE LLAMA SAY TO OTHER BEFORE THEIR HOLIDAY? ALPACA MY BAGS.	WHAT DO YOU CALL A COW THAT CAN'T PRODUCE MILK? AN UDDER FAILURE.
WHAT DO YOU CALL A RESTAURANT THAT ONLY SERVES RUSSIAN GANGSTERS? RED MOBSTER.	WHAT DID THE SNOWCONE SAY WHEN HE GOT HIS VISION BACK? ICEY!

WHAT'S A SKELETON'S FAVORITE FORM OF ART? SKULL-PTURES.	WHY DON'T BLIND PEOPLE EAT FISH? BECAUSE THEY CAN'T SEAFOOD.
WHAT DID THE CANADIAN EAGLE SAY? "I'M SOARY."	WHAT'S THE SMELLIEST HAIR? NOSE HAIR.

WHAT UNIT OF MEASUREMENT IS USED FOR SNAKES?	WHY WASN'T THE COMPUTER HUNGRY?
INCHES, THEY DON'T HAVE FEET.	HE JUST HAD A BYTE.
WHAT'S A MARGARITA LOVER'S FAVORITE BOOK?	WHAT KIND OF PERSON WEARS TWO WATCHES AT ONCE?
TEQUILA MOCKINGBIRD.	SOMEONE WITH TOO MUCH TIME ON THEIR HANDS.

WHAT STORES HAVE THE MOST PROBLEMS?

MAGAZINE STORES. THEY ALWAYS HAVE ISSUES.

WHY DO BIRDS FLY SOUTH FOR THE WINTER?

IT'S TOO FAR TO WALK.

WHY WAS THE BROOM LATE?

IT OVERSWEPT.

HOW DO YOU KNOW HOW HEAVY A RED HOT CHILI PEPPER IS?

GIVE IT A WEIGH, GIVE A WEIGH, GIVE IT A WEIGH NOW...

WHY DID THE COWBOY ADOPT A MINIATURE DACHSHUND?

BECAUSE HE WANTED TO GET A LONG LIL DOGGIE.

DID YOU HEAR ABOUT THE NEW RESTAURANT THEY OPENED ON THE MOON?

FOOD'S GREAT BUT THERE'S JUST NO ATMOSPHERE.

WHY DO ITALIANS LIKE SHARP ANGLES?

BECAUSE THEY'RE ACUTE.

WHAT'S BROWN AND STICKY?

A STICK.

WHAT DID THE INSULATION SAY TO THE HOUSE?

"NO GUARANTEES, BUT I'LL DO ASBESTOS I CAN."

WHAT DO YOU CALL A BLIND DEER?

NO EYE-DEER.

WHAT IS FORREST GUMP'S PASSWORD?

1FORREST1.

WHAT KIND OF CLASSICAL MUSIC DO CHICKENS LISTEN TO?

BACH, BACH, BACH.

WHAT DO YOU CALL A NOSE WITHOUT A BODY? NOBODY KNOWS.	HOW DO DOGS PARTY? THEY RAISE THE WOOF!
WHY DO COWS HAVE BELLS? BECAUSE THEIR HORNS DON'T WORK.	HOW DOES MOSES MAKE HIS COFFEE? HEBREWS IT.

WHY DIDN'T THE MAN LIKE CIVIL WAR JOKES?

HE DIDN'T GENERAL LEE FIND THEM FUNNY.

WHY DID THE COFFEE TASTE LIKE MUD?

IT WAS FRESH GROUND.

WHAT SHOULD YOU DO IF SOMEONE CALLS YOU ODD?

GET EVEN.

DID YOU HEAR ABOUT THE KIDNAPPING AT SCHOOL?

DON'T WORRY HE WOKE UP.

WHAT'S THE LAZIEST PART OF THE CAR? THE WHEELS, BECAUSE THEY'RE TIRED!	WHAT IS THE COLDEST COUNTRY IN SOUTH AMERICA? CHILE.
WHAT KIND OF SHOES DO ARTISTS WEAR? SKETCHERS.	WHAT POOLS ARE SAFE FOR DIVING? DEEP ENDS.

WHAT KIND OF LIGHTS DID NOAH HAVE ON THE ARK?

FLOODLIGHTS.

DO YOU HAVE A BOOKMARK?

YES, BUT MY NAME IS BRIAN.

WHY DO GOLDFISH LIKE TO HIDE IN PONDS?

THEY ARE JUST BEING KOI.

WHY DID THE BLIND MAN FALL DOWN THE WELL?

HE DIDN'T SEE THAT WELL.

HOW DID THE HIPSTER BURN HIS MOUTH? HE DRANK HIS LATTÉ BEFORE IT WAS COOL.	HOW DOES A JEDI SING ON THE MOUNTAINS? HE YODALS!
WHAT DO YOU CALL A FISH WITH NO EYES? A FSH.	WHY CAN'T YOU HAVE A NOSE THAT IS 12 INCHES LONG? THEN IT WOULD BE A FOOT.

WHAT DO YOU CALL A LOBSTER WITH A CHRISTMAS HAT?

SANTA CLAWS.

HOW DO YOU MAKE TISSUE DANCE?

YOU PUT A LITTLE BOOGIE IN IT.

WHY DID THE MINER NEED GLASSES?

HE HAD TUNNELVISION.

WHY WILL KIM JONG-UN NEVER USE NUCLEAR WEAPONS?

HE'S AFRAID IT WOULD COST HIM HIS KOREA.

WHY DO MOON ROCKS TASTE BETTER THAN EARTH ROCKS?

BECAUSE THEY'RE METEOR.

WHAT DO YOU CALL A WATERFOWL THAT LOOKS IN YOUR WINDOWS?

A PEKING DUCK.

WHAT DO YOU CALL A BIRD THAT IS AFRAID OF HEIGHTS?

A CHICKEN.

IS THERE AN ADVANTAGE TO LIVING IN SWITZERLAND?

NO, BUT THE FLAG IS A BIG PLUS!

HOW DID PEOPLE APOLOGIZE BACK IN THE DAY?

THROUGH REMORSE-CODE.

WHAT DID THE JANITOR SAY WHEN HE JUMPED OUT OF THE CLOSET?

SUPPLIES!

WHY IS THERE A FENCE AROUND CEMETERIES?

BECAUSE PEOPLE ARE JUST DYING TO GET IN.

WHAT DID THE VEGETABLES SAY AT THE PARTY?

LETTUCE TURNIP THE BEET!

WHAT IS THE DIFFERENCE BETWEEN A HIPPO AND A ZIPPO?

ONE IS REALLY HEAVY, AND THE OTHER IS A LITTLE LIGHTER.

WHY WAS THE ROBOT ANGRY?

SOMEBODY KEPT PUSHING HIS BUTTONS.

WHAT DID THE NUT SAY WHEN IT WAS CHASING THE OTHER NUT?

I'M A CASHEW.

WHY ARE ELEVATOR JOKES SO GOOD?

BECAUSE THEY WORK ON SO MANY LEVELS.

WHERE DOES THE LONE RANGER TAKE HIS TRASH?

T'DA DUMP T'DA DUMP T'DA DUMP DUMP DUMP, T'DA DUMP T'DA DUMP T'DA DUMP DUMP DUMP.

WHAT DO YOU CALL A FUNNY MAN FROM AFRICA?

MALARIOUS.

WHAT DOES A CAT SAY WHEN ITS MOUTH HURTS?

MEOWWTH.

WHAT'S A PALINDROME?

NO IT ISN'T.

WHAT GOES "OOOO" "OOOO"? A COW WITH NO LIPS.	**WHAT'S THE FRIENDLIEST ANIMAL IN THE OCEAN?** A "CUDDLE" FISH.
WHY SHOULDN'T YOU LIKE GIRAFFES? THEY ARE INTALLERABLE.	**WHAT DID BABYCORN ASK MAMACORN?** "WHERE IS POPCORN?"

WHY WAS THE MEXICAN FOOD COLD?

BECAUSE IT WAS A LITTLE BRRRRRRRITO.

HOW DO YOU KNOW WHEN YOU'RE DROWNING IN MILK?

WHEN IT'S PAST YOUR EYES.

HOW OFTEN SHOULD YOU TELL JOKES ABOUT CHEMISTRY?

PERIODICALLY.

WHY WERE ALL THE DOGWOOD TREES SILENT?

THEY LOST THEIR BARK.

WHY WAS THE CELLPHONE WEARING GLASSES?

BECAUSE HE LOST ALL HIS CONTACTS.

WHAT DO YOU CALL THE SECURITY OUTSIDE OF A SAMSUNG STORE?

GUARDIANS OF THE GALAXY.

WHAT'S THE DIFFERENCE BETWEEN A GOOD JOKE AND A BAD JOKE TIMING?

WHEN DOES A JOKE BECOME A DAD JOKE?

WHEN THE PUNCH LINE BECOMES APPARENT.

WHY DO I TELL DAD JOKES?

BECAUSE THAT'S HOW EYEROLL.

47787360R00073

Made in the USA
Middletown, DE
10 June 2019